James Field Stanfield

The Guinea Voyage

A Poem

James Field Stanfield

The Guinea Voyage
A Poem

ISBN/EAN: 9783744712620

Printed in Europe, USA, Canada, Australia, Japan

Cover: Foto ©Thomas Meinert / pixelio.de

More available books at **www.hansebooks.com**

James Field Stanfield

The Guinea Voyage
A Poem

ISBN/EAN: 9783744712620

Printed in Europe, USA, Canada, Australia, Japan

Cover: Foto ©Thomas Meinert / pixelio.de

More available books at **www.hansebooks.com**

THE

GUINEA VOYAGE.

A

POEM.

IN THREE BOOKS.

BY

JAMES FIELD STANFIELD.

———————

LONDON:

Printed and Sold by JAMES PHILLIPS, George-Yard, Lombard-Street,

M.DCC.LXXXIX.

T H E

P R E F A C E.

THE author of the following poem having given to the world a little tract, intituled, " Obfervations on a Gui- " nea Voyage," had no intention to trouble the reader with a preface; but conceiving that the prefent work might fall into hands which the other had never reached, he thought it proper to fay, that it was made up not from hearfay, and the communi- cation of others, but from his own experience, (poetical figures excepted) in confequence of an actual refidence on the coaft of Africa, and the performance of a Guinea voyage.

He now fubmits his little effort to the publick, and fhall feel himfelf amply repaid, if he can intereft the feelings of but a few individuals in fuch a manner, as to fecure their attention, and occafion them to reflect upon the fubject.

May the 8th 1789.

a   ARGUMENT

ARGUMENT OF THE FIRST BOOK.

ADDRESS to the muſe.—Drearineſs of the ſubject, and difficulty of expreſſing it in its true colours.—Aſſociation of merchants, and outfit of the voyage.—General difficulty, and artifices uſed, in obtaining a crew.—Some, from the pangs of unrequited paſſion, ruſh voluntarily into the trade.—Such the caſe of Ruſſel—his character and tale.—Character of the maſter of the veſſel.—The crew obtained—take leave of their connexions and ſail—paſs by Madeira—and Canary Iſlands.—Exclamation to the winds.—Barbarity towards the ſeamen begins to make its appearance.—Apoſtrophe to Britiſh ſeamen to avoid the trade.

ARGUMENT OF THE SECOND BOOK.

THE veſſel approaches the coaſt.—The Guardian Genius of Africa calls a council of the other preſiding powers—deſcribes to them the miſeries occaſioned by European viſitors—

and

and proposes to each of them in his department, to rouze the different demons of the climate, and arm them to punish the invaders on board the approaching vessel.—They obey her mandate.—The morbifick plagues crowd to the vindictive standard, and, taking death for their leader, stand embattled on the shore.—The vessel arrives and anchors.—Native-agents are allured, and go out on the business of the voyage.—Slaves are brought down to the vessel—are examined—purchased—put on board—and confined below.—Death, at the head of his legions, beholds the scene.—Dispatches Cruelty from the ranks to take possession of the master's heart.—Effects of this union on the crew.—The whole pestiferous body advance to the attack.—Progress of the sickness among the crew.—Death of Russel.—The contagion spreads.—Dishonours of the dead.—Address to the British senate.

ARGUMENT OF THE THIRD BOOK.

BENEVOLENT example of the Quakers proposed — The Middle Passage commences.—Night view of the slaves below.—Morning scene, when brought upon deck.—Time for messing arrives.—Some refuse sustenance, and perish.—Story of

Abyeda.—Child-birth on the paſſage.—Addreſs to the Bri-
tiſh ladies.—The ſlaves arrive in the colonies—are ſold by
ſcramble—are ſeparated from their connexions, and landed.—
Addreſs to Divine Juſtice—efforts of mercy.—Abolition of
the ſlave trade anticipated—prophetick view of Africa after
the abolition.

THE

THE

GUINEA VOYAGE.

BOOK THE FIRST.

THE direful voyage to Guinea's sultry shore,
And Afric's wrongs indignant Muse! deplore.
The Muse, alas! th' opprobrious theme disdains,
And starts abhorrent from th' unhallow'd strains.
How blest the bard whom happier themes inspire,
Who wakes with kindred lays his melting lyre;
Whose liquid tones by sympathy impart,
Joy's glad emotions to the feeling heart!
O far from me the notes which pleasure sings!
With trembling rage I sweep the harsher strings.
My grating shell shou'd wound the tortur'd ear,
For discord only can be music here.
Be mine such deadly notes as fiercely pour
The shrieks of anguish on the midnight hour!
Be mine the broken strain, the fearful sound,
That wildly winds the howling death-song round!

Come

Come then, O heav'nly Mufe! with Sybil-bough,
Lead thro' the horrors of thefe fcenes of woe:
Support the fainting weaknefs that recoils
At well-known griefs, and long-fupported toils:
Extend thine hand where threat'ning gulphs are fpread;
Lift thy broad fhield where ftorms beat round the head:
Illume the dreary wafte—infpire the lay—
Guide my weak pow'rs along the arduous way:
Help me to paint the melancholy view,
The difmal track of ocean to purfue,
And with the Eagle-eye of Truth pervade
All the dark mazes of th' *inhuman Trade.*

O could the verfe but to my wifhes move,
No fpicy zephyrs borne on wings of love,
No gentle pinions, fanning fpring-tide air,
Should give one image, or be mentioned here.
Thy black *Tornado*, ill-ftar'd *Afric*—thine—
Should be the model of my varied line!
On the ftill diction of the mournful ftrain,
The rifing darknefs fhould profufely reign:
The fable cloud fhould wrap the fullen fong,
And in grand melancholy fweep along:
Then, by degrees, with gath'ring horrour fraught
Tempeftuous numbers, and electric thought,
Shake the big thunder—dart th' indignant beam—
Till the full torrent pour'd the headlong ftream,

Whelm'd

Whelm'd ev'ry burfting breaft in twofold ire,
Grief's melting fhow'r—and indignation's fire.

At length the harden'd merchants clofe combine,
And midnight Council broods the black defign ;
Strikes the firft link of the tremend'ous chain,
Whofe motion vibrates thro' the realms of pain.
Th' infatiate thirft of av'rice to fupply,
Or fill the pomp of fancy's changing eye,
For vice, intemp'rance, paffion, to provide,
To drefs up folly, or to pamper pride,
The dev'lifh *traffic*'s plann'd.   Now bufy care
Furrows each face, and clamours rend the air.
The founding anvil fhakes the diftant main,
Forging with pond'rous ftrokes th' accurfed chain.
Th' attractive *outfit* claims each buftling hand :
Confufion works, and uproar gives command.

But arduous moft (and that which moft prevails,
And day and night th' unwearied mind affails)
Of Neptune's fons a dauntlefs crew to gain,
To fteer their veffel through the boift'rous main.
For this a tribe confed'rate take the wing,
And round refiftlefs youth their poifons fling.
Polluted dens of infamy they throng,
With painted vice, to raife the Syren-fong ;
With fpecious arts fubdue th' unwary mind,
Then clofe their web, and faft their victims bind.

At length with debts fictitious charge their cafe,
And make a *dungeon* ftare them in the face.

Shut now from comfort, agoniz'd with grief,
Hopelefs alike of juftice, or relief————
One only portal opes the gloomy road ;
One dire condition burfts the drear abode.
Slav'ry's dark genius heaves the iron door,
And, grinning ghaftly, points to *Guinea*'s fhore————

The mad'ning wretch now leaves the prifon gate,
And feels with horror his approaching fate.
Some few, the voluntary woe embrace,
Sore from falfe friends, or undefcrv'd difgrace ;
Subdu'd by pow'r, by fell misfortune worn,
Or by the pangs of hopelefs paffion torn ;
Weary of griefs no patience can endure,
They feek the *Lethe* of a mortal cure.

Such, *Ruffel*—lov'd companion, faithful friend !
Such were thy motives, fuch thy purpos'd end.
Thy harmlefs fpirit—gentleft of thy kind,
Was ne'er to favage cruelty inclin'd,
Long happy *Afric* would have feen her fons
Crowd freedom's plains, beneath protecting thrones ;
E're thy meek hand—in virtue only brave,
Had put one fetter on the proftrate flave !

Far other feelings his mild foul impreft ;
Far other ardours fhook his hopelefs breaft.

With

With pureſt paſſion long his boſom beat,
Its riſe propitious, and its progreſs ſweet.
Returning love diffus'd the namelefs charm,
And met his hopes, in virgin bluſhes warm.
In mutual confidence and fondneſs bleſt,
No guilt alarm'd, nor fear diſturb'd the breaſt.
But eyes parental, film'd with doubtful hue,
(That with inverted glaſs youth's proſpects view,)
Mark'd the ſoft tranſports of their chaſte delight,
And peeviſh envy ſicken'd at the ſight.
With keen infliction giv'n, the ſtern command
Cut with relentleſs ſtroke the tender band.
The pious maid, with duteous, fearful ſmart,
Tore the fond lover from her trembling heart.
Deſpairing, doating—with diſtracted mien—
He flew the ſpot, and chang'd the heav'nly ſcene;
Ruſh'd to the rigours of the frozen Pole,
To quench the conflicts of his fervid ſoul:
His fervid griefs the frozen aid deny,
And brave the winter of an arctic ſky;
Thence by the winds and fiercer paſſions blown,
He tries the ardours of the flaming zone.
Seeking with hopeleſs agony to find
Extremes like thoſe, which ſhook his tortur'd mind;
From cold deſpair's keen night and icy ſway,
To all the ſcorchings of Love's burning ray.

See

See o'er the gloſſy wave the veſſel ſkim,
In ſwelling garments proud, and neateſt trim,
Glitt'ring in ſtreamers, deck'd in painted guile,
Cov'ring the latent bane with ſpecious ſmile,
In ſhining colours, ſplendidly array'd,
Aſſume the honours of an *honeſt trade*,
And hide, beneath a proſtituted glare,
The poiſon'd purpoſe, and th' inſidious ſnare.

The crew for once now raiſe th' aſſociate ſtrain,
And the laſt drops from pleaſure's goblet drain.
The gloomy *maſter* views with looks malign
Their ſhort-liv'd mirth, and hugs the black deſign——
Feeds his dark rancour with the foul alloy——
How ſoon the impending fate will damn their joy.

So when primeval bliſs through *Eden* ſtream'd,
And young-ey'd innocence on pleaſure beam'd,
With heedleſs joy the unſuſpecting pair,
Revell'd in guiltleſs rapture, void of care.
Stung with the ſight, the foul-enſnaring fiend,
Slav'ry's firſt author, with fell rancour grinn'd ;
Fermenting envy ſwell'd the villain-thought—
How ſoon his kindred mates, with malice fraught,
Sin, pain, and *death,* would throw their ſhades between,
And blaſt with horror the delightful ſcene,
Change the lov'd converſe and th' enchanting air,
To ſhrieks of woe and howlings of deſpair !

Now

Now toft beneath the veffel's ample fide,
The laft boat lingers on the breaking tide.
The bending deck receives the parting crow'd ;
And fhades of forrow ev'ry face o'ercloud ;
Affociates, friends, comprefs the burning hand ;
In pale dejection weeping maidens ftand—
Prefageful, eye the liquid, wild abyfs,
And wet with tender tears the trembling kifs ;
Sink from the nervelefs arm, in loft difmay,
As the dread fignal fpeeds the boat away ;
Three foul-expanding fhouts the fkies divide ;
Three wild, refponfive cheers re-echo wide—
The fweet vibrations tremble on the ear
The laft delightful founds they'll ever hear !
And now the refluent boat evades the fight,
High-mounting waves the veffels difunite.
Still the white fignal, fading, ftrains the eyes,
Still the lorn lover with his hand replies ;
Till melting into air—the object loft—
And duty fternly calling to his poft,
'Twixt him and joy th' eternal curtain's drawn,
No more of blifs to know another dawn.

Swift from the breezy north, affifting gales
Impel the courfe, and fwell the yielding fails.
Before the fightlefs breeze the veffel flies,
Clambers the mountain fea, and braves the fkies ;

Or

Or thund'ring down the depths that foam below,
Ploughs up the frothy brine with dafhing prow.
The rattling cordage whirls, the fail-yards ftrain,
The winding pipe re-echoes o'er the main :
Firm in their ftations, ply th' obedient crowd,
Trim the directing lines, and ftrain the fhroud;
Tug at the beating fheets with finew'd force,
And give the vaft machine its fteady courfe.

    Now, all that meets the vainly ftraining eye,
Is boundlefs ocean and unmeafur'd fky.
Unlefs perchance, beyond the wat'ry trace,
Iberia's purple hills th' horizon grace :
Or on the right, with a whole vintage red,
Storm-beat *Madeira* waves her woody head.

    Still o'er the pathlefs wafte, with rapid force,
Led by th' encreafing ray, we urge the courfe.
Surrounding dolphins gambol o'er the tide,
And deck the blue-green wave with filver pride:
Swift from the beauteous tyrant, the weak fry
Forfake the flood, and arid æther try,
Spread the moift wing—attempt th' untoward height,
And in fhort foarings urge their trembling flight.
The breathing porpus cleaves his pond'rous way,
The flouncing fkipjacks bound in liquid play;
Bonitoes court the fpray on either fide,
And Albicores in fhining mazes glide :

While

While huge Leviathan, in monarch mood,
Spooms, like an iſland, thro' the ſubjeƈt flood.

　At length aſſiſted by the boreal breeze,
And ſouthward urg'd by ſwift-purſuing ſeas,
Cloſe in our liquid path blue mountains riſe,
Lifting their miſty ſummits to the ſkies ;
The cluſt'ring iſles, (once fortune's own domain)
That break the ſurges of th' *Atlantic* main.

　Next on our left, rear'd by volcanic fires,
Shading all ocean, *Teneriffe* aſpires,
Above the topmoſt clouds, with giant might,
Heaves his *Promethean* peak to ſeize the light,
And thro' conduƈting veins, with chemic pow'r,
Recruits exhauſted nature's fiery ſtore.
While from the Weſt ambroſial ſcents exhale,
As *Palma* ſhakes her orchards to the gale.
Up from the rocky beach the cluſters run,
And ſpread their purple ripeneſs to the ſun.

　Theſe ſcenes, alas ! we paſs with luckleſs ſpeed,
And all their beauties rapidly recede.
For, from the mazy chambers of the ſky,
Loos'd by chill *Boreas*, all the breezes fly ;
And from the pole with force gigantick hurl'd,
Urge our ſwift paſſage through the wat'ry world.

　Unconſcious winds, why waft your ſpeeding gales ?
Why breathe your influence on the ruffian ſails ?

Is

Is it yon enfign, waving high in air,
With *Britifh* crimfon dy'd, that claims your care ?
Alas ! unconfcious winds—yon waving red,
With *Britifh* honours fo profanely fpread,
Is not the hallow'd ftandard, whofe high fame
Leads *Albion*'s fons to deeds of proud acclaim ;
Is not the flag, with whofe protecting fway
Commerce embolden'd tries the watry way.
Beneath that fpecious banner, the dark pow'r
Of favage rigour ripens ev'ry hour :
The bloating poifon fwells the feeble bound,
And burfting throws the rankled venom round.
    Now reftlefs tyranny triumphant reigns,
For now no profpect of retreat remains.
Far from fair freedom's blifsful regions thrown,
The mournful feamen heave th' unheeded groan.
At ev'ry movement of th' imperious brow,
Beneath rude hands, the haplefs victims bow.
Should difcontent be feen, or angry eye,
Struck to the deck the proftrate fuff'rers lie :
Or to the fhrouds inglorioufly bound,
They feel the lafh in many a fmarting wound.
Nor can refentment lift th' avenging hand—
With funken fpirits, and a frame unmann'd—
For (now the meal in ftinted fcraps fupplied,
And cheering bev'rage purpofely denied.)

The

The vital current flags—th' finews faint,
Th' exhaufted voice fcarce breathes the weak complaint:
A torpid languor feizes ev'ry vein,
And the foul finks beneath th' oppreffive chain.

   Ye fons of *Britain*, who, in dangers brave,
Dare all the tumults of th' uncertain wave;
Whofe dauntlefs minds alike with ardour glow,
To waft fair commerce, or to meet the foe;
O fhun the fatal courfe!—the torrid ray
Will wither elfe each active pow'r away:
Unnerv'd at length the common fate you'll meet,
And gafp refiftlefs at your tyrant's feet.
Then with the laft-drawn groan of deep defpair
You'll curfe the day that gave you vital air!

END OF THE FIRST BOOK.

THE

GUINEA VOYAGE.

BOOK THE SECOND.

HIGH, where primeval forefts fhade the land,
    And in majeftic, folemn, order ftand,
A facred ftation raifes now its feat
O'er the loud ftream, that murmurs at its feet,
Of *Niger*, rufhing thro' the fertile plains,
Swell'd by the cataracts of tropic rains,
Long 'ere furcharg'd his turgid flood divides,
To burft on ocean in three thund'ring tides.

    Thither high-feated in an iv'ry car,
Glitt'ring with gold exprefs'd in many a ftar,
By alligators drawn in dread array,
Afric's aërial emprefs bends her way.
The fpicy breezes throw their fweets around ;
With pealing ftrains the hollow woods refound :
A train of nymphs furround the radiant pow'r,
And duteous lead her to the regal bow'r.

Amidft

[13]

Amidſt the ſplendours, that thus round her ſhone,
Th' imperial miſtreſs fill'd the Sylvan throne.
Th' Heſperian ſun from the deſcent of day
Beam'd on her front ſerene a languïd ray.
About her ſandal'd feet, in ſapient mood,
The river-gods, an awful council, ſtood :
And ev'ry pow'r, that rul'd the burning clime,
Sat in the crowded court with port ſublime :
When round th' auguſt Divan a mournful look
Caſt the ſad Queen, and thus the ſilence broke.

Ye various rulers of th' extended ſhores,
Where bounteous day his brighteſt radiance pours ;
On whoſe ripe vales the fat'ning deluge flows,
Luxuriance ſits, eternal ſummer glows ;
Say, can ye longer brook the ſavage hand,
That, with rapacious av'rice, thins the land ?
Can ye reſiſtleſs ſee the ruthleſs chain
Still ſpread its horrors o'er th' unpeopled plain ?
Look over yonder main that ſhakes the ſhores,
Where yon green-promontory's ſummit ſoars,
The tawny ſail our ſurging bulwark braves,
(Cruel the winds, and treacherous the waves)
Europe's pale ſons direct the barb'rous prow,
And bring their ſtores and inſtruments of woe.

Say, ſhall theſe tyrants with inhuman aim
Our hapleſs ſons and weeping daughters claim ?

Shall

Shall we—O blind !—ftill aid the ruffian band,
That ftains our coaft, and bares our wretched land ?
Our realms, alas ! abandon'd to defpair,
Supinely funk, the flavifh fhackles wear :
Surges in vain defend the burning ftrand ;
In vain impervious forefts fence the land.
Our native monfters treach'rous tamenefs fhew,
Forget their fury, and admit the foe ;
Our rebel crocodiles their fiercenefs lofe,
Shrouding their treafon in the gelid ooze ;
Our ftinglefs ferpents twine in gentle play,
And harmlefs tygers crop the flow'ry fpray ;
The recreant lion fmooths his favage eye,
While the dire fpoiler ftalks unheeded by.
Fly to your fep'rate realms, ye chiefs of worth,
And call the vengeful pow'rs of *Afric* forth ;
Summon difeafe, with all her ghaftly brood,
To greet thefe traffickers in human blood.
Call forth the terrors of the fervid fkies ;
Bid mifty demons from your marfhes rife ;
With congregated horrors crowd the plain—
And drive thefe pallid robbers o'er the main !
   An awful murmur inftantly tranfpires—
Th' applaufe, that wifdom gives, when genius fires ;
Not the vain fhout the fhallow rabble draws,
But confcious judgment's well-approving paufe.

Nor

Nor with weak praife they greet the fcepter'd fair,
But fpeed to execute th' important care.
   Now thro' the dufky air they range their flight,
Veil'd by the cov'ring of the baleful night.
To thoufand realms the charge vindictive flies :
In thoufand realms their fummon'd furies rife ;
To the dark ftores of pain they fly to arm—
And, there prepar'd, the dreadful legions fwarm.
   Red from the foggy eaft the fun afcends,
And gleams new terror on th' envenom'd fiends :
Round their ghaunt leaders throng th' unfightly hoft,
Rear the black fign, and fill th' allotted poft.
In heavy columns troops *lethargic* found,
Flap their huge wings, and throw their opiates round.
Fierce o'er the field conflagrant fquadrons bend,
And fiery *fevers* thro' the regions fend.
While from moift clouds, which brood o'er defarts bare,
Where *Lambre*'s ftagnant lake pollutes the air,
Prefs frigid *agues* in th' alternate row,
And give their chill variety to woe.
   But chief—the multitude that crowds the field,
That points the fpear, and lifts the Gorgon fhield,
Breaks from the flimy marfh and fwampy plains,
Where proud *Benin* in triple bulwark reigns.
Call'd by the zenith fun, the putrid band
Spreads its corrofive poifons o'er the land :

Myriads

Myriads of fprites their acrid venoms throw,
And *colic* arrows fly from ev'ry bow.

Rang'd in broad horror, with extended line,
In dread battalia the grim fpectres fhine ;
Unnumber'd, gory ftandards wave around,
And fhrieks and groans (their native mufic) found.
But now, a dreadful paufe—fpread wide and far—
Throws more than terror o'er the baleful war.
Such dreadful paufe fhall frighted nature feel,
'Ere the laft trump refounds th' eternal peal.
For full in front, bedew'd with orphan's tears,
Their ghaftly leader, Night-born *Death* appears.

Mean while the turgid blafts the fails expand,
And drive the veffel to the deftin'd land ;
Anchor'd at length, and pafs'd the wat'ry way,
She opes her luring treafures to the day ;
Such treafures as beguile the favage mind,
And leave no marks, but thofe of vice, behind.

Quick the deluded natives wing their way,
And prowl infatiate for the deftin'd prey.
Unfeeling *av'rice* helps t'extend the wound,
And flyly hurls the flaming brand around.
See—his fell torches fpread devouring fires !
The peaceful village in the blaze expires.
Sunk in the terrors of their burning rage,
Lie helplefs *infancy* and feeble *age* ;

While

While *Vigour*—flying the confuming ray,
'Scapes but to drag in chains the ling'ring day.

Nor thefe the only ills that haunt the fhore,
And fpring deftructive from the freighted ftore.
The hind returning from his daily care,
Seiz'd in the thicket, feels the ruffian fnare.
Mean while his anxious wife, with eager eye,
Looks on the homeward path, and evening fky.
Children, bereft, the nightly boon require,
And anxious call their flow-returning fire.
Ne'er fhall returning fire his children blefs——
Ne'er fhall the weeping wife her hufband prefs——
For av'rice, burfting ev'ry tender band,
Sweeps, like a deluge, thro' the haplefs land!

Slow to the fhores now march the fetter'd crowd,
Tugging their chains, or bent beneath the load.
Torn from all kindred ties difmay'd they ftand,
While prying cruelty's infulting hand
Minutely vigilant, with butcher fkill,
Turns the dejected victim at it's will,
And (ev'ry limb, and ev'ry joint furvey'd)
Completes the practice of the brutal trade.

Now the fad purchafe—Heav'ns! my pow'rs refufe,
Tho' truth illumines, and tho' fires the mufe.
Nature recoils, and in her depths profound,
Receives, heart-ftruck, the parricidal wound!

C

As

As the wan traders pay *the price of blood*,
O'er the black profpect gathering terrors brood :
The guardian fpirits look with horror down,
And change their mattins to one hideous groan.
E'en the bright angel, fent t' enrol the deed
By heav'n born *Juftice*,—turns afide his head ;
And as th' infernal crime his fingers trace,
Hides, with his fnowy veft, his tortur'd face.

   The purchafe made, in fable terrors dreft,
The fhip receives each agitated gueft.
Torn as his bofom is, ftill wonder grows,
As o'er the vaft machine the victim goes,
Wonder, commix'd with anguifh, fhakes his frame
At the ftrange fight his language cannot name.
For all that meets his eye, above, below,
Seems but to him the inftruments of woe.
The yawning deck now opes the dreary cell;
Hot mifts exhale in many a putrid fmell.
Confin'd with chains, at length the haplefs flave,
Plung'd in the darknefs of the floating cave,
With horror fees the hatch-way clofe his fight——
His laft hope leaves him with the parting light !

   This faw the ghaftly chief, as on the fhore,
He waited with his hoft th' avenging hour ;
Quick, from the ranks he calls a blood-nurs'd fiend,
Hell fees no direr from her womb afcend :

'Twas

'Twas on a rack the monfter held his ftand ;
A fcorpion fcourge wav'd in his wither'd hand ;
Snaky his locks—his eye-balls roll'd in flame ;
Sin's fecond-born, and *Cruelty* his name.

Fly, fays the night-born chief, without delay,
To where yon veffel rides the wat'ry way.
Upon the *mafter* all your influence pour,
And join with him to fpeed th' avenging hour,
Soon fhall my fiends your red-ftain'd track purfue,
And clofe the carnage on the ruffian crew.

The mandate giv'n, quick from the rack he flies,
And to the *mafter* turns his ftedfaft eyes ;
Down, like the lightning's fury, rufhes prone,
And on his heart erects his bloody throne.

Infpired thus, and thus his heart poffeft,
New tumults kindle in his flaming breaft.
Pallid or *black*—the *free* or *fetter'd* band,
Fall undiftinguifh'd by his ruffian hand.
Nor age's awe, nor fex's foftnefs charm ;
Nor law, nor feeling, ftop his blood-fteep'd arm.
While, fkill'd in ev'ry torture that can rend,
O'er gafping heaps exults th' affociate fiend.

Mark, how in hellifh wantonnefs, he calls
Yon trembling innocent—the fight appals !
The weeping facrifice, with nervelefs pace,
Obeys the mandate—while his infant face

The

The butcher feizing, with infernal hold,
Haftens his gripe in lacerating fold ;
In his torn mouth the wounded paffage finds,
And thro' the mangled cheeks his fingers winds !
 This but his firft effay. Infpir'd anew,
He feeks frefh tortures for his trembling crew.
Convolv'd in pangs, that rev'rend form furvey
Beneath his country's wars and commerce grey,
Now writhes his tortur'd frame ! The fcourges ply—
And from the lafh the quiv'ring morfels fly.
 Invention next, from her exhauftlefs ftores,
O'er the bare bones the venom lotion pours,
Whofe acrid falts in fearching conflict dart,
With pungent anguifh barbing ev'ry fmart :
The tortur'd fibres their laft feeling ftrain,
And life juft vibrates on the ftrings of pain !
 Nor this the clofe : between his toothlefs jaws
The furious monfter the thwart iron draws——
The poor relief to wail his fate denied,
And the hot gore fent down in choaking tide,
Unnat'rally return'd with horrid force,
Dire meal ! again to throb its wafted courfe !
 But while new tortures raife the piercing cry,
And wound with dreadful fight the wearied eye,
Th' avenging hour arrives—in dreadful din
The troops of wan difeafe their march begin.

With

With eagle eye they trace the fatal road
Their agent *cruelty* had mark'd with blood.
Death, ghaftly death, the fable ftandard bears,
And at their head in all his pow'r appears.

Now droops the head in faint dejection hung,
Now raging thirft enflames the dry parch'd tongue;
In yellow films the raylefs eye is fet,
With chilling dews the loaded brow is wet;
Fierce thro' the burning roads of purple life,
The various venoms rufh with rival ftrife,
Their poifons thro' th' inteftine mazes bear,
The vifcous linings from their channels tear;
Pour with corroding deluge thro' the frame,
And whelm the vitals in the liquid flame.

Th' infected air, upon her loaded wings,
Thro' the warm fhip the green contagion flings.
Strew'd o'er the filthy deck, the fever'd lie,
And for cool moifture raife the feeble cry;
The pitying meffmate brings the cheering draught,
And, in the pious act, the venom'd fhaft,
Repays the charity with barb ingrate,
And whelms the foother in the kindred fate.

Three mifty funs in beamlefs grief arofe,
And glimmer'd, *Ruffel*, on thy mortal woes!
The fourth beheld th' eternal angel nigh,
As friendfhip fpeechlefs watch'd thy fading eye.

While

While throbs convulfive thy ftrain'd vitals wrung,
One only murmur trembled on thy tongue,
One fov'reign accent rack'd thy parting frame—
The rending founds, that form'd *Maria*'s name !
And as thy laft pulfe beat with quiv'ring chill,
Thy trembling eye-balls look'd *Maria* ftill.

 The gloomy King in joy infatiate ftrides,
And o'er the havock dreadfully prefides ;
No fpeedy exit to the fuff'rer fhews,
But makes him linger out his painful woes.
In livid clouds the fallow fkin is vein'd.
With putrid fores the ghaftly form is ftain'd :
The palfied limbs refufe their wonted aid ;
'Midft filth and blood the meagre body's laid ;
Hunger's fell worm tugs with inceffant rage,
And arid thirft, no potions can affwage :
Corrofive pain prolongs the wrankling wound,
'Ere franchis'd life can leap the burning bound,
All that with anguifh can afflict the mind,
With all that racks the dying frame conjoin'd.

 Nor does the flaming fword of vengeance fheath,
Tho' the laft pang be paid to victor death.
O'er the fall'n reliques new difhonours brood ;
Unholy fury rends the facred fhroud ;
If to the fea confign'd—the hallow'd corfe
The briny monfters feize with favage force.

If

If to the frefh'ning flood the lifelefs clay,
Rank alligators feize the quiv'ring prey.
Or when, more favour'd, on the burning land
The kindred duft is mix'd with folemn hand,
Fierce from his nightly watch and native wood,
Lur'd by the diftant fcent of morbid blood
The tiger rufhes by foul carnage led,
From the frefh tomb tears up the the reeking dead,
Devours the mangled limbs—churns the chill gore——
The laft avenger of th' infulted fhore !

Like the wild fcreaming of the midnight blaft,
'Midft the torn cordage of the fhatter'd maft,
With notes that pierce th' unwholfome welkin through,
The fhrill-blown pipe convenes the remnant crew.
The remnant crew their o'ercharg'd bofoms fmite,
And rife to join the melancholy rite.
With painful fteps the burning deck they crowd,
Or penfive hang upon the flacken'd fhroud ;
Speechlefs they mark the foul prefageful wave,
That, *Ruffel*—parting, opes thy fluid grave !

The jutting hatch, a fable bier, is laid,
The pitchy pall throws a funereal fhade,
His honour'd corfe in awful form difpos'd,
Decent his clay-cold limbs—his eyelids clos'd ;
The ringlet dear, which once *Maria* grac'd,
Upon his breaft by holy friendfhip plac'd ;

The

The finking iron flung with duteous pains,
In fhrouded canvafs wrapt his cold remains,
A rev'rent filence the fad profpect draws ;
The facred liturgy, with folemn paufe
Swells the fad found, at whofe *inverted* doom,
Plung'd in th' abyfs, he finds the liquid tomb !
   O ye, who form the Senatorian band,
And help to guide the councils of the land,
Say, can ye hear thefe tales of mortal woe,
And bid your tears forget their tafk to flow ?
Are there among you, whofe exalted plan
'Tis to affwage the fufferings of man ?
Are there, who, proud of Britain's publick name,
Pronounce her navy. fountain of her fame ?
Are there fincerely good among her fons
And that there are exulting Britain owns ?
O timely join your fympathetick aid
To blaft the horrors of th' infernal trade !
So fhall your bufts each refcu'd infant prefs,
Mothers unborn for living fons fhall blefs.
So fhall pofterity to lateft age
Engrave your names upon her faireft page,
And weave a crown, to thofe alone decreed,
Who refcue *millions* by one glorious deed.

END OF THE SECOND BOOK.

THE

GUINEA VOYAGE.

BOOK THE THIRD.

BLEST—ever bleft, remain the gentle band!
  Whofe peaceful fpirits and whofe Chriftian hand,
Have loos'd the fetters of the captive race,
And bid fair freedom feize oppreffion's place.
Friends be their well-earn'd name, emphatic given,
Friends to mankind, and delegates of heaven!
No frantic wars difgrace their mild abodes;
Nor rigour bends, nor felfifh guile corrodes;
Nor impious oath their pure affirmance ftains;
Peace lights their gentle path, and wifdom reigns.
Freedom, fimplicity, religion's rays
Combin'd, reftore *Aftræa's* golden days.
O would mankind the bright example view,
Prefs the fmooth track, the godlike aim purfue!
Would they conjoin'd the virtuous purpofe aid,
Soon the black vitals of th' opprobrious trade

D

Would

Would fail, foon ceafe the blood-disfigur'd fcene,
The captive's woe, the victim's trembling mein,
And all the ills (a lamentable train)
That now demand the renovated ftrain.

The hateful purchafe made——compreffive ftow'd,
The floating dungeon with th' unnat'ral load
Is cramm'd profane : immers'd in deadly gloom,
The fhackled fufferers wait th' expected doom,
Till the bark, glutted with the purchafed gore,
Hoifts the full fail, and quits the wafted fhore.

Now from the fcanty crew the goblins dire
Avert a while the dart : the fiends require
A fuller carnage. On the haplefs train,
T' avenge whofe wrongs they left the burning plain,
They turn infatiate ; and with recreant rage,
On the chain'd fufferers wars atrocious wage.

Soon as umbrageous night on raven-wings
O'er the fad freight her dewy opiates flings,
Pack'd in clofe mifery, the reeking crowd,
Sweltering in chains, pollute the hot abode.
In painful rows with ftudious art compreft,
Smoking they lie, and breathe the humid peft :
Moiften'd with gore, on the hard platform ground,
The bare-rub'd joint foon burfts the painful bound ;
Sinks in th' obdurate plank with racking force,
And ploughs,——dire tafk, its agonizing courfe !

Nor

Nor can they turn to an exchange of pains,
Preſt in their narrow cribs, and girt with chains,
Th' afflictive poſture all relief denies,
Recruiting ſleep the ſqualid manſion flies,
In one long groan the feeble throng unite ;
One ſtrain of anguiſh waſtes the lengthen'd night.

    With broad'ning diſk, and ſlow increaſing ray,
Up from old ocean climbs the orb of day.
Then the drear hatchway morning hands diſcloſe,
And point the ſufferers to a change of woes.

    Soon as the gorged cell of dim diſeaſe
Opes the ſick paſſage to a quicker breeze,
From the rank maw, belched up in morbid ſteam,
The hot miſt thickens in the ſide-long beam ;
When from the noiſome cave, the drooping crowd,
In fetter'd pairs break through the miſty cloud|
With keen deſpair they eye the morning's glow,
And curſe the added day that ſwells their woe.
Wet with foul damps, behold the ſad array
Diſcloſe their mis'ry to th' unpitying day.
Look at yon wretch (a melancholy caſe !)
Grief in his eye, deſpair upon his face ;
His fellow—ſee—from orbs of blood-ſhot ire
On his pale tyrants dart th' indignant fire !

    Striving with feeble force to preſs the grate,
Yon ſtruggling ſuff'rer heaves a pond'rous weight.

Stripes

Stripes from the founding lafh, fierce drawn, fucceed,
To give the fainting trembler haplefs fpeed.
Alas! the founding lafh applies in vain ;
For clofe united by the feft'ring chain,
His dead companion up th' untoward height,
(Struck by the mortal minifters of night)
The living victim tugs with painful throes ;
Himfelf, lefs bleft, referv'd for keener woes.
 Now hot black clouds in fpreading volumes rife :
Now culinary uproar fhakes the fkies.
Spread through the venom'd fhip, with buftling care,
A joylefs meal the tyrant-whites prepare.
Marfhal'd around th' unwifh'd-for mefs they lie,
And the ftrange nutriments difcons'late eye.
Sunk with dejection, fome the viands fpare,
Some with keen fcorn reject the proffer'd fare,
Keep the fuperior pride, that nerves the brave,
Nor, free-born, tafte the portion of a flave.
But fee the fcourge, that fpares nor fex nor age,
Stripe follows ftripe, in boundlefs, brutal rage.
See the vile engines in the hateful caufe
Are plied relentlefs ; in the ftraining jaws
The wrenching inftruments with barbarous force
Shew the detefted food th' unwilling courfe.
But vain are torments ; fenced by deathlefs bounds
Beyond the reach of agonizing wounds,

'Midft

'Midſt adamantine bulwarks thron'd ſerene,
Immortal *freedom* holds ſuperior reign ;
Smiles from the heights of his eternal tower
On tyrant's malice, and oppreſſion's power.

 In the thick gloom of yonder penſive ſhade
Is loſt *Abyeda*'s wretched form diſplay'd,
Abyeda, once among the vocal throng
The theme and miſtreſs of each rural ſong :
Once the blithe leader of each feſtive ſcene,
That woke the muſic of the joyous green.
Ne'er did ſuch nymph before her brightneſs lave
Within *Formoſa*'s deep, tranſlucent wave.
O'er her ſmooth form grace threw her waving line,
And beauty wandered in the rich deſign.

 Unrivall'd long had liv'd the happy maid ;
And many a hero had her love eſſay'd.
But youthful *Quam'no* was the virgin's pride ;
Her friend, protector, and her faithful guide.
Faſt by her ſide he kept his guardian way,
Leſt treach'rous *Whites* ſhould ſeize the tempting prey.
The freſh'ning cocoas from their height he bore,
Cluſt'ring bananas ſpread their juicy ſtore,
The ſpotted ſpoils too deck'd her rural bow'r,
When from the chace, in the dear ev'ning hour,
Glowing, ſhe met him with the welcome ſmile ;
Pleas'd, and yet anxious at the manly toil.

And

And now through dewy dawn, the rifing ray
Lights up the radiance of their bridal day.
With early nymphs within the bufy room,
Amidſt the labours of the flying loom
Of vivid tints ſhe plied the various thread ;
The long-plann'd work, to grace the nuptial bed.
With beating ſteps refounds the hollow floor ;
To rapid ſtrokes refponds the clam'rous door.
With breathlefs energy ſhe flies amain,
To meet her *Quam'no* and the bridal train.
Alas ! no *Quam'no* meets her eager eye—
In rufh the fpoilers with detefted cry, ?
Seize with rapacious force the trembling prey ;
And to the ſhore the haplefs maid convey.

　When urg'd by rage, or hunger's burning force,
The rav'ning lion darts his furious courfe,
And through the num'rous herd undaunted goes ;
So *Quam'no* rufhes through the crowd of foes.
Carves his fierce way, entwines the fainting maid ;
But vain protection ;—lo ! a treach'rous blade,
Darted behind him with unerring aim,
Impales him deep ; convuls'd the bleeding frame,
Plunges indignant o'er the tainted ground,
Life rolls his torrent through the yawning wound,
O'er his fierce eyes death's hideous ſhadows move
With fable veil, and ſhut out light and love.

Abyeda

Abyeda now upon the lifeless form,
Sinks in despair beneath the trying storm.
The murd'rous stroke that mark'd his early tomb,
Involves her intellects in deadly gloom.
Her wounded reason the sad mansion flies :
Sense wanders widely, and reflection dies !
   Now (scourges having long their fury spent)
Gloomy and sad, beneath oppression bent,
Round her gall'd neck the fest'ring iron winds,
And to the gloomy mast oppressive binds.
Sad strains of feeble melancholy flow ;
Half-meaning fragments of recorded woe,
In wild succession break the pensive lay,
Through the drear night and lamentable day.
Her sad associates lift the melting tones,
And join each cadence with according groans.
But sick'ning nature with the burden reels ;
O'er her wan face the deadly jaundice steals ;
The spirits die ; the nerveless limb's unstrung ;
With mortal gripe the wounded heart-string's wrung ;
Fix'd her sunk eye—her love-lorn ditty fails,
Life beats tumultuous 'gainst the feeble pales—
Convulsive throbs expel the final breath,
And o'er the fatal close sits ghastly death.
   Hark ! from yon lodge in many a wounding groan
A lab'ring fair one raise the feeble moan !

Swift

Swift to the darkfome cell the females fly,
To ftill the tumult of th' expected cry :
Join the deep woe with one combin'd exclaim ;
As pangs maternal fhake her drooping frame.
Heav'ns ! what a manfion for the tender woes,
The painful travail partial nature throws
Upon the gentler fex—When lenient art
And foothing care fhould cheer the fainting heart,
Here, with dejected wretchednefs enclos'd,
To brutal hands and impious eyes expos'd,
Her facred forrows the fad crifis prefs,
Occurrent horrors, premature diftrefs,
Spread with foul clouds the inaufpicious ray,
That opes the new-born victim's doleful day !
  Behold her bending o'er her infant charge,
Hear the laments her copious grief enlarge.
" Ill-fated innocent (fhe wailing cries)
" Thou joy and anguifh of thefe aching eyes,
" Of parent mifery the haplefs heir,
" Thy mother gives the welcome of defpair ;
" Greets thy unconfcious fmile with throbbing fears ;
" Repays thy fondnefs with prefageful tears.
" Where now the joys fhould light the holy bow'r ?
" Where the fweet hopes that wings the natal hour ?
" Nor hope's bleft dawn fhall e'er thy fancy warm ;
" Nor joy's fweet fmile e'er cheer thy mortal-form.

No

" No father hails thee with a confcious pride;
" Thy future worth no flatt'ring friends decide :
" A wretched mother prefs'd by tyrant fate,
" Can yield no fuccour to thy helplefs ftate :
" The fpoiler's chains, that load her languid frame,
" By fpoiler's right thy fetter'd fervice claim."
 For ev'ry virtue fam'd, ye Britifh fair,
Can ye this foul reproach unheedful bear?
O rife aufpicious, lead the lib'ral train,
That aims to fhake oppreffion's iron reign.
A nation's councils oft' your pow'r obey;
The wars of nations own your fov'reign fway.
In foft humanity's congenial courfe,
Your kindling charms will claim refiftlefs force:
When beauty lifts her eye in mis'ry's caufe,
Compaffion wakes, and follows with applaufe.
 Fainting with fuch a courfe of loathfome views
And length of horrors, the dejected mufe
Spreads her tir'd wings, and, with defponding mien,
Flies o'er the clofe of the deftructive fcene;
Sees the dire bark 'midft direr regions fteer;
Hears the plung'd anchor tell grim flav'ry near;
Beholds the fell receivers quickly pour
In favage fwarms upon the blood-ftain'd fhore,
Sees them approach with all their ftore of chains,
To load (curft act!) oppreffion's weak remains.

E

Now

Now o'er the gloomy ſhip, in villain guiſe,
The ſhrouding canvaſs drawn, ſhuts out the ſkies.
The pitchy curtain throws a ſhade between,
(Meet apparatus for the horrid ſcene,)
Rang'd all in rows, and ſtation'd at command,
In trembling ſtate the wretched victims ſtand ;
And dumb and almoſt lifeleſs they await
The dreadful ſignal that's to mark their fate.
  With cords now furniſh'd, and the impious chain,
And all the hangman-garniture of pain,
Ruſh the dread fiends, and with impetuous ſway,
Faſten rapacious on the ſhudd'ring prey.
What ſhrieks of terror reach the ſick'ning ſkies,
What floods of anguiſh drown their wounded eyes,
As ſtrife tumultuous ſhakes the *ſcrambling* brood,
Scrambling for *human fleſh—for kindred blood!*
Struck with diſmay, ſee yonder fainting heap !
Yon ruſhing group plunge headlong in the deep !
(With the fierce blaſt extinct the vital fires)
Yon falling maid, ſhrieks—ſhivers—and expires,
As in cloſe folds the fated victims cling,
Their circling cords the ruffian agents fling ;
Tear from the lock'd embrace the weeping ſpoil,
As av'rice marks it capable of toil ;
And binding into lots the ſtruggling band,
Drag them ferocious to the waſteful land.

Now

Now in the furge is dipp'd the bladed oar,
And wafts a boat-load to the guilty fhore.
One dreadful fhriek affaults th' affrighted fky,
As to their friends the parted victims cry.
With imprecating fcreams of horror wild,
The frantick mother calls her fever'd child.
One univerfal tumult raves around;
From boat to fhip refponds the frantick found:
And flies with tenfold anguifh to the throne,
Where *juftice* fits, and calls the thunder down.
. Immortal King! in whofe impartial eye,
Nor clime, nor realm fuperior ftate enjoy.
No worm-rais'd ftation warps thy juft decree,
No tinctur'd fkin's a prejudice to thee;
But to thy fov'reign care the various frame
Of men and nations finds an equal claim!
How long wilt thou th' afcending cries withftand!
How long retain the thunder in thine hand?
Or doft thou rather from the horrid fcene
Turn thy relenting eye to the foft mien
Of proftrate *mercy*; who, with ftreaming eye
Arrefts thy wrath, and puts the tempeft by.
Haft thou difpatch'd her, rob'd in virgin white,
Thy joyful delegate from realms of light?
Ah! yes; I fee her tread the favour'd land:
I know the meek-eyed pow'r; fhe takes her ftand,

Where

Where the *felected few*, with fapient care
The gen'rous aims of *liberty* prepare.

The facred delegates from freedom's throne
Through Afric's foil fpeed the commiffion'd boon.
Quick through the joyful land the tidings ring ;
Rejoicing crowds th' enfranchis'd bleffing fing.
Science awaken'd leads the free-born ftrain ;
And arts and commerce follow in the train.
Rear'd by protecting laws new cities rife,
And heave their turrets to the lucid fkies.
Trade lifts his trident o'er the filver tide,
New harbours opens, bids his navies ride ;
Sees, unpolluted by oppreffion's hand,
His honeft wealth ftream through the joyous land ;
His crowded quays heap'd with the guiltlefs toil,
Iv'ry and gold in many a burnifh'd pile,
Drugs, fpices, gums, in rich profufion thrown,
And all the treafures of the torrid zone.
Culture emergent o'er the damafk plains
Spreads her rich veft, and gaudy Flora reigns.
Where marfhes once difplay'd their fickly green,
Health lifts her rofeat face, and points ferene
The cot, where mild Content with confcious grace
Smiles on her hufband Labour's glowing face.
Pierc'd by no funs, th' interminable wood,
Whofe pathlefs gloom fcreen'd horror's drear abode,

Opes

Opes its long viſtas to the cheerful loves :
And nymphs and ſylvans in the ſcented groves
(Where demons us'd to haunt the thorny ſhade)
Aſſemble blithe, and ſweep th' unfolded glade.

In freedom's train, the ever foremoſt band,
The jocund muſes ſkim the happy land.
Sweet *Poeſy* precedes the virgin quire
Calls Inſpiration with her ſounding lyre :
Gives to awaken'd verſe th' auſpicious morn,
Whoſe mid-day fire ſhall quicken bards unborn.

In the full ſuffrage of immortal ſtrains
The future *Hayley* of theſe ſolar plains,
Warm'd by the theme, will ſhake the tuneful ſhores,
From Gambia's flood to mild Angola's bow'rs.
His heav'n-born lay will fire th' enraptur'd throng,
While neighb'ring realms hang o'er the ſacred ſong,
That ſings, How wafted from the genial iſle,
Whoſe ſilver clifts on circling ocean ſmile,
Looſe-veſted liberty, by *Mercy* led,
Broke the huge chain, preſs'd *Slav'ry*'s miſcreant head,
Bad reſcu'd Nature claim her birth-right boaſt ;
And *Britiſh* freedom ſmile on *Afric*'s coaſt.

F I N I S.

www.ingramcontent.com/pod-product-compliance
Lightning Source LLC
Chambersburg PA
CBHW021444090426
42739CB00009B/1639